The Greek Gods Guide
To Depression & Mental Illness

Dying is Easy. Living is Hard

**By
Christopher Strauss**

Copyright © 2025 Chris J. Strauss

All Rights Reserved

ISBN: 979-8-218-83066-3

Table Of Contents

Dedication i
Acknowledgment ii
What To Do First 1
    Talk To Someone 1
    You Are Not Alone 1
Chapter 1 - Meet The Roman Goddess Of Misery 2
    A Lesser-Known goddess 2
Chapter 2 - My History With Mental Illness 4
Chapter 3 - Greek Myths That Explore Mental Illness 5
Chapter 4 - The Maze In Your Mind And Your Own Personal Minotaur .. 9
    The Maze and the Minotaur: 9
Chapter 5 - What is Depression 14
    Know Your Enemy: 14
Chapter 6 - Depression and Your Brain 16
    Physical Effects of Depression 16
Chapter 7 - Neurotransmitters and You 18
    The Hermes Messengers Of the Brain: 18
Chapter 8 - How Depression Changes Your Brain 19
    Physical Changes: 19

Chapter 9 - Talk Therapy and You 21
    Talk Therapy 21
Chapter 10 - 3 Steps To Make Changes In Your Mental Health Journey. 23
Chapter 11 - Balance & You.. 25
Chapter 12 - What is Happiness?... 28
Chapter 13 30
    Philosophy 30
Chapter 14 35
    Protein's Effects On Serotonin & Dopamine: 39
Chapter 15 41
    Sleep & Mental Health 41
Chapter 16 43
    Chasing the Runners' High 43
Chapter 17 44
    Meditation & Mindfulness:... 44
    Meditation:.. 45
    Mindfulness Bell - A 5-Minute Mindfulness Meditation: 45
    Meditation Research:... 46
    Improve Serotonin Levels:.. 47
Chapter 18 48
    Your Personal 12 Trials To Recovery 48
Chapter 19 50
    Dying Is Easy, Living Is Hard... 50

Chapter 20 51
    About The Author... 51
References... 52

Dedication

I dedicate this book to the Green power ranger JDF.

Once a ranger always a ranger.

Acknowledgment

To my mentor Chasen for introducing me to buddism and meditation when I needed it.

What To Do First

Talk To Someone

Substance Abuse and Mental Health Services Administration

SAMHSA's National Helpline: 1-800-662-HELP (4357) or text 988 for the Suicide Support line. They are available 24 hours a day and seven days a week.

Before you start reading, let me know that you can overcome any mental anguish or concern you have with time and effort. It may not be easy, but it is possible with the right motivation.

You Are Not Alone

National Institute of Mental Health. In 2022, their study showed that 23.1% of people living in the United States had one diagnosable mental illness.

What does that mean then?

That means that over 59.3 million people in the U.S. are going through the same kind of mental anguish you are experiencing.

Before you do anything rash, like acting out or self-harm, please call the number above first.

It is best to talk to a professional trained in psychology and mental illness, who will help you understand what you are going through and provide help.

Chapter 1 - Meet The Roman Goddess Of Misery

A Lesser-Known goddess

Miseria is the Roman goddess of **Depression**, **Anxiety**, and **Grief**. The word misery comes from Miseria, which we all know too well.

Why Do the gods Care:

One thing that mythical gods realize is that a world of corpses can't worship them. They must work on balancing the world to prevent it from imploding.

Miseria's job is to balance the world's depression, anxiety, and grief and to keep them in check with the rest of the mythical gods' schemes.

The Roman god of war, Mars, may promote warfare in the real world, but Mars must also keep a balance and prevent a nuclear war. If we destroyed the world, no one could worship the gods.

Inspiration of the gods:

Like the mythical tales of ancient Greek heroes, the gods were known for helping the chosen few worthy of their wisdom and support.

The goddess's self-interest is in keeping a balance in the world's mental health.

The goddess is encouraged to inspire doctors, scientists, and psychiatrists to help find peace in this chaotic existence.

For me, she is inspiring me to write this book to help others find a level of relief and hope for a continued existence with mental illness.

She is telling me to write this book. To help others find the kind of relief and structure that has gone a long way to helping me live an improved life with mental illness.

Chapter 2 - My History With Mental Illness

My interpretation of "Depression" is a heavy weight that sits in my chest and only grows more severe with every negative thought or action. Like many College Freshmen, my mental health struggles started in college, living in the dorms. I was having trouble socializing with my fellow students. My socializing problems led to isolating myself and not seeking social companionship.

My thoughts wandered into a train of introspection, which disassembled all my life mistakes and found even more errors or hardships to add to the dumpster fire of my life.

I started to experience "Magical Thinking," like out-of-control thoughts about how the news or media influenced me to do outrageous things. I had unbelievable abilities, like infiltrating computers or finding meaning in random events.

My thoughts kept getting darker and darker over time, which led to thoughts of self-harming and wanting to kill myself.

After several episodes of self-harming and trying to kill myself, I was able to get the help I needed. Unfortunately, this included dropping out of college and seeking counseling and medical interventions like medication to help me cope and deal with my depression.

Chapter 3 - Greek Myths That Explore Mental Illness

The ancient Greeks were a nation of philosophy and a deep understanding of the world. They used myths as a tool to help the public understand the world. The following Greek myths have a deeper meaning that can assist you in understanding mental health.

Sisyphus

Sisyphus was the King of Corinth who ruled his kingdom with an iron fist.

His first transgression was when Zeus, the king of the gods, was angered when Sisyphus killed visitors and travelers in his palace. Willfully killing royal guests or foreigners violated Greek hospitality rules. Zeus also felt betrayed when he abducted the river god Asopus's daughter Aegina, a water nymph. Sisyphus had told the river god of the culprit and where he could find Asopus's daughter.

Zeus then ordered the god of death, Thanatos, to chain Sisyphus in Tartarus's underworld once the king had died. When Thanatos, the god of death, appeared to Sisyphus on his deathbed, he showed the dying king the chains he would wear in Tartarus for eternity. Being crafty, Sisyphus first asked the god of death to demonstrate how the chains work. While Thanatos showed how they go around his wrist, Sisyphus pounced on him, locking the chains tightly around him.

With the god of death in chains, this meant that no one could die anymore.

Sisyphus had invertedly made everyone on Earth immortal, which angered the gods.

Ares, the god of war, was the most upset since his battles had no meaning if the soldiers didn't die. Zeus then ordered Ares to free Thanatos and return mortality to the world.

Once Sisyphus had died for a second time, he arranged for his wife to throw his body in the river and not perform any funeral rites for him. Not performing funeral rites was taboo in Greek culture, and Sisyphus pleaded with Hades' wife, Persephone, to be let out of the underworld to haunt his wife. He was allowed out of the underworld for three days and then required to return. Of course, Sisyphus missed that deadline and was able to resurrect himself in the land of the living.

Zeus, of course, wanted to send Thanatos to drag him back to the underworld, but because of their last encounter, he didn't like to risk getting put in chains again. Now that Sisyphus was back in the land of the living without fear of reprisals, he again lived to a ripe old age and died a third time of natural causes.

Once Sisyphus had died for a third time, Zeus was done playing around with him and wanted a special punishment in the underworld. Hades, the god of the underworld, crafted an eternity of Sisyphus pushing a boulder uphill. Before he reaches the top of the hill, the boulder rolls back downhill, forcing him to start over again.

Sisyphean is the term for denoting or relating to a task that can never be completed.

The Meaning of Pushing a Rock Uphill

Pushing a rock uphill is just like the average job or chores you go through every day.

A student gets up in the morning to go to school and has homework and tests to deal with. Daily work is just like pushing a boulder up the hill, as every task makes the student push the boulder and move it up the mountain.

When the day ends and we sleep, the boulder rolls down the hill to start the cycle again.

The size of your boulder depends on the amount of work and responsibilities you have to deal with.

The average child only deals with schoolwork and home life, which means they most likely have a relatively light load, no more different than pushing a beach ball up a mountain.

An average parent must manage a job, raise children, and manage a household. These responsibilities can make their load more formidable, but it is no different than pushing an actual boulder uphill.

When you introduce depression and mental illness into the mix, things only get worse. Depression only adds to your load, making it harder to push your boulder uphill. What was easy one day only continues to get worse and worse. When you cannot move your boulder up the mountain, it is no different than seeing your daily life implode as you just want to remain in bed. The world just flashes by as you are not motivated to deal with life.

Chapter 4 - The Maze In Your Mind And Your Own Personal Minotaur

The Maze and the Minotaur:

The Greek Myth

Synopsis

The Greek Island nation of Crete was a regional powerhouse in ancient times that had power over Athens. Crete's king, Minos, would sacrifice his prize bull calf yearly to keep the favor of the god of the sea, Poseidon. Then, one year, Minos had such a lovely and prized bull calf born that he didn't want to sacrifice it to Poseidon, so he sacrificed a lesser bull calf.

Of course, not sacrificing the prize bull calf upset Poseidon, and to get his revenge, Poseidon had the goddess of love, Aphrodite, make Minos's wife, Queen Pasiphae, fall in love with the prized bull.

The Queen goes to their chief engineer, Daedelus, to help her create a costume that will make her look like a female bull so that she can mate with the prized bull. Daedelus designs a wooden structure on wheels with cow skin to help the Queen pose like a female bull in heat in the pasture. Nine months later, the Queen gives birth to a half-man, half-bull abomination they named the Minotaur.

Soon after this, the king's son, Prince Androgeus, competes in the Athenian Olympic Games and is envied for his strength and speed, making him the champion of many events.

Being a champion caused a lot of jealousy among the other contestants. After a night of drinking wine at a tavern, a fight broke out, and Prince Androgeus was slain. The death of a Crete prince on Athenian soil would typically mean war, but King Minos instead provided a method of compensation to avoid war.

King Minos declared that when the full moon is on the equinox every nine years, Athens will send seven young virgin men and women to be sacrificed to the minotaur in its labyrinth. This regular cycle of sacrifice would continue until the beast was dead.

Theseus is the prince of Athens and is also part god, as Poseidon slept with his mother. He is a demigod of beauty and the strength of a god. He was determined to slay the minotaur and end this cycle of sacrifice.

When the ship carrying the sacrifices arrived at the island of Crete, the Cretan Princess Ariadne gazed upon Theseus and instantly fell in love with him.

While the prince was a prisoner, she talked to Adriadne, and it became clear that Theseus intended to kill the Minotaur. She agreed to assist him with the promise that the Prince would marry her.

The Princess immediately asked Daedalus, the architect of the vast underground labyrinth, for help. Although the architect did not love the Cretan king or the Minotaur, he was happy to give her a ball of twine.

As the day of sacrifice had finally arrived, the King's soldiers marched the young men and women to their deaths. Once locked into the labyrinth, Theseus waited as the other men and women entered the vast corridors of the maze. He tied the end of the twine string to the entrance and walked through the dimly lit corridors. The walls echoed with the horrible screams of the sacrifices as the beast attacked and feasted on their flesh. The passageways were flush with the scent of rotting flesh. Theseus carefully explored the tunnels, following the screams.

As Theseus started to get closer to the minotaur, he saw the beast in the dim light.

Feasting on the fresh corpse of a young woman, the Prince lightly stepped up to the beast with his hidden dagger in hand. With a savage scream, he leaped onto the back of the beast, thrusting his dagger repeatedly into the back of the horrific beast.

The beast tried to resist as Theseus drove his dagger into its flesh. Driving the dagger home into the monster's heart, it slumped on the top of his latest sacrifice as his blood mixed with his victim's.

Now that the beast was dead, Theseus led the remaining sacrifices to the maze entrance, using the twine as a guide. Since the Minotaur was dead, the cycle of sacrifice was over, and Theseus could return to Athens with his new bride.

What does the maze represent?

Our minds are a complex maze of thoughts and memories that tremendously influence our lives. Like the Minotaur, we all have those negative thoughts that pull us into despair. We call them our demons that whisper negative thoughts and make us want to hurt ourselves and others.

Sometimes, we can keep the beast at bay, but all too often, our personal Minotaur plunges us into a pit of despair. As your life spirals out of control, the beast's whispers worsen. The only question is whether you give the Minotaur demon the power to harm yourself or others.

Even though you may slay the beast and quiet your mind for a time, the beast remains in the dark corners of your mind.

> *"Information is power."*
>
> - *Francis Bacon*

Now, how do you cage the depression beast?

> *"Asking for help is a sign of strength, not weakness."*
>
> - *Brené Brown*

Now, who do you turn to first?

In ancient times, people sought support from a wise man, a holy person, or a healer.

In today's world, we call them medical doctors; your family doctor is a good place to start.

Your family doctor will be able to run medical tests to see if there is any medical reason for your depression. A doctor can include looking for any physical damage to your head or chemical deficiency in your body.

The doctor will also know your available talk therapy and medication resources, such as counselors and psychiatrists.

Chapter 5 - What is Depression

Know Your Enemy:

The Merriam-Webster Dictionary Defines Depression as:

- An act of depressing or a state of being depressed, such as a state of feeling sad: low spirits: melancholy

Specifically: a mood disorder that is marked by varying degrees of sadness, despair, and loneliness and that is typically accompanied by inactivity, guilt, loss of concentration, social withdrawal, sleep disturbances, and sometimes suicidal tendencies. See also clinical depression, major depression, and postpartum depression:

(1) a reduction in activity, amount, quality, or force, a depression in trade

(2) biology: a lowering of physical or mental vitality or of functional activity

If you feel like you have experienced this for more than two to fourteen days, please:

Talk To Someone:

Substance Abuse and Mental Health Services Administration

SAMHSA's National Helpline: 1-800-662-HELP (4357) or text 988 for the Suicide Support line. They are available 24 hours a day and seven days a week.

Chapter 6 - Depression and Your Brain

Physical Effects of Depression

We all have our definitions of depression and how it affects us. What is it doing to us physically and chemically, and what can we do about it?

Like any disease that does damage to the human body, depression is no different. There are material changes to the brain that will most likely only get worse without intervention. Extensive research has gone into understanding the brain and the changes caused by depression. You can find the following information on the Mayo Clinic website.

https://www.mayoclinic.org/

Know the Field of Battle:

A Simple Understanding of the Brain:

Billions of nerve cells are arranged in patterns that coordinate thought, emotion, behavior, movement, and sensation. A complicated highway system of nerves connects your brain to the rest of your body so that communication can occur in seconds.

Brain Structure:

- **Neurons:**

A nerve cell (neuron) communicates with other cells through electrical impulses when the nerve cell is stimulated. Within a neuron, the impulse moves to the tip of an axon and causes the release of neurotransmitters, chemicals that act as messengers.

- **Neurotransmitters:**

Neurotransmitters pass through the synapse, the gap between two nerve cells, and attach to receptors on the receiving cell. This process repeats from neuron to neuron as the impulse travels to its destination — a web of communication that allows you to move, think, feel, and communicate.

- **Neurotransmitters and Depression:**

The National Institutes of Health

The monoamine-deficiency theory posits that the underlying pathophysiological basis of depression is a depletion of the neurotransmitters serotonin, norepinephrine, or dopamine in the central nervous system. Serotonin is the most extensively studied neurotransmitter in depression.

Chapter 7 - Neurotransmitters and You

The Hermes Messengers Of the Brain:

Types of Neurotransmitters:

Serotonin is a natural body chemical that controls mood. It works with melatonin to help regulate sleep and wakefulness, pain, well-being, and sexual desire. Medicines that increase serotonin levels can help with depression.

Cortisol is a steroid hormone produced by your two adrenal glands, which sit on top of each kidney. When you are stressed, increased cortisol enters your bloodstream. The right cortisol balance is essential for your health; producing too much or too little cortisol can cause health problems.

Dopamine is a neurotransmitter in the brain associated with pleasure, reward, motivation, and motor control. In psychology, it's linked to feelings of gratification and is implicated in mood disorders, addiction, and specific behaviors when its levels are imbalanced.

Norepinephrine increases arousal and alertness, promotes vigilance, enhances memory formation and retrieval, and focuses attention. It also increases restlessness and anxiety.

Chapter 8 - How Depression Changes Your Brain

Physical Changes:

There are two critical structures in the brain that Depression can deform:

Amygdala:

The amygdala is the part of the brain most closely associated with fear, emotions, and motivation. Its name means "almond" because it is almond-shaped. If you see something frightening, your amygdala might tell your body to panic.

Depression causes an increase in the size of the Amygdala, and this may correlate with an increase in anxiety during depressive episodes. (1)

Hippocampus:

The hippocampus is involved in memory, learning, and emotion. Its most significant job is to hold short-term memories and transfer them to long-term storage in our brains. It also plays a role in emotional processing, including anxiety and avoidance behaviors.

Depression decreases the amount of grey matter in the Hippocampus, and this may correlate with a decrease in cognitive and memory skills during depressive episodes. (2)

Chapter 9 - Talk Therapy and You

We all have to start somewhere.

We all need a safe place to discuss everything on our minds Regardless of how messed up or demented your thoughts What you talk about is between you, the counselor, and God.

Talk Therapy

Counseling is always an excellent place to start. (3,4).

Finding a mental health specialist to talk to, rather than any friends or family members, is always essential. Speaking from experience, you will have thoughts so personal, disturbing, and embarrassing that you would not share them with those you care about.

A mental health counselor is required to keep anything you talk about confidential and cannot share anything you talk about.

The only two things that will cause the counselor to report anything are if they feel that you are a threat to yourself or someone else.

This way, you have a safe place to discuss the kind of dark and disturbing thoughts that you have going through your mind regularly.

By talking to a professional counselor, you can explore the problems you are experiencing.

Medication Options:

Finding the proper medication to help balance your mind. Finding the right Doctor for your needs. A psychiatrist is a medical doctor who specializes in treating depression and mental illness...

The psychiatrist will first be able to schedule various medical tests to determine any physical reason for your mental anguish.

Medications for depression and mental illness have come a long way over the years. You and your psychiatrist will be able to explore what kind of medication you need.

Your family doctor will be able to recommend a psychiatrist in your area.

Chapter 10 -
3 Steps To Make Changes In Your Mental Health Journey

Discover the center of your mental health crisis and address it.

Why?

The first question you should ask when suffering from any crisis:

I was becoming too socially isolated in my college dorm, and that was causing me to feel depressed and alone. I had no social outlet to discuss fellow interests, gossip, or discuss current events. I didn't have any real friends, which was drowning me in a pit of despair that took time to escape.

1. *Once you know the "Why," you will want to address the problem head-on.*

It wasn't until I started making friends again and socializing that I could address my social issues. Thankfully, I had old friends who got me involved in Dungeons and Dragons-style role-playing games. We often catch the latest movies and hang out at our favorite buffet restaurant.

These are the kinds of questions that you can discuss with your mental health counselor to help you explore the mental health crisis and gain a level of control.

2. *Explore the best lifestyle changes to help address your mental health concerns.*

These changes, in addition to medication and talk therapy, can help determine what you need to help manage your mental health. These changes can be anything from getting more exercise to reading a good book or talking to a friend.

3. *Find the balance.*

One thing you learn about mental health is what your limits are and when you need to find a balance between work and play. Find out the amount of stress and energy you can apply to your daily life before your mental health worsens.

"All Work And No Play Makes Jack A Dull Boy,"

- *Stephen King from The Shining (1980)*

Chapter 11 - Balance & You

Finding a Balance.

The Myth of Icarus

The boy who flew too close to the sun.

The architect of the Minotaur Maze, Daedalus, was imprisoned with his son Icarus to protect the Minotaur Maze's secrets. The father-son duo was in the prison tower and had no hope of being let out. The tower had a platform at the top that Daedalus and Icarus had access to.

The top of the tower was a popular roost for pigeons and various other birds that provided a large amount of discarded feathers.

Daedalus had access to his tools and woodworking equipment, so he conceived wings using wax, a wooden frame, and the leftover pigeon feathers. He knew this was the only way to get freedom for himself and his son, Icarus.

Once Daedalus had completed the wax wings, he prepared to fly away. In preparation to fly away, Daedalus gave his son two rules.

Rule #1:

Do not fly too close to the sun.

Candle wax has a low melting point, and getting too close to the sun would melt his wings, causing him to fall to his death.

Rule #2:

Do not fly too close to the water surface.

The sea spray would weigh down the wings, causing him to crash into the sea and drown. The day soon came when Daedalus and his son would launch from the top of the tower with their wax wings. At midday, they jumped off the building and soared, leaving their prison far behind.

They felt like gods soaring through the skies, only to realize they must follow their own rules. At first, Daedalus noticed that Icarus was gaining altitude, flying too close to the sun.

For Icarus, flying was invigorating. He wanted to fly higher, not concerned with getting too close to the sun. As he felt like a living god and soared through the heavens, his wings melted, leading to his crash back to the earth.

Daedalus could only look on as his son, who would not listen to his pleading to fly lower, watched as his son Icarus fell to his death. He could only continue with his flight to his freedom and mourn the death of his son.

Meaning

Breaking down the meaning.

We will first want to look at the ocean's meanings.

Ocean

1. If you do too little, you will fail.

Sun

    1. If you do too much and burn out, you will fail.

It is all about finding the balance in life.

If you do nothing in life, like your daily self-care or going to work, you will only drown in your filth and poverty.

Sun:

If you do too much in life, like working ten-hour days, managing a household, and working a second job, you will only burn yourself out. You will not take the time to care for your emotional and physical needs. You will want to learn how to manage your time and balance work and play.

Once you know what your limits are, you will be able to plan for your future.

Finding that balance can also make you want to search for happiness in your everyday life. Most enter college after high school to develop their job skills and get the job of their dreams.

However, developing a mental illness such as depression, anxiety, or something similar can throw a pretty big wrench in those plans. So, how do you find your happily ever after and see what you need to achieve the ultimate goal we all strive for?

Chapter 12 - What is Happiness?

Happiness

A state of contentment and well-being, or a pleasurable or satisfying experience

Merriam-Webster Dictionary

> *"The secret of happiness, you see, is not found in seeking more, but in developing the capacity to enjoy less."*
>
> ***Socrates***

Poor mental health can lead to failing grades that destroy your academic career. My depression symptoms were the big reason I took a break from my academic studies to concentrate on my mental health. Once I could better manage my mental health in the next couple of years, I resumed my studies and got a bachelor's Degree in Social Work and minored in Psychology. Being able to move back with my family helped me develop the support I needed to create healthy mental health.

Developing mental health problems will make you evaluate the next steps in your life. Enjoying less can mean anything, like avoiding alcohol when you go out with friends or avoiding stressful situations. You will want to discover the best path to developing a healthy mind and lifestyle.

Treating your mental health is more difficult when you are still in grades 1 - 12, waiting to graduate from High School. Again, this is when you will want to evaluate how best to address these issues. Your school should have a counselor or academic adviser who can help develop a plan for helping you work on your mental health and succeed in school.

Now, what do you do when you are past college or working a full-time job? Working with a mental illness can be the most difficult, considering you are most likely one of the primary financial resources for yourself or your family. Dealing with a mental illness can put a strain on your finances. These are the first things you will want to discuss with your mental health specialist. You will want to see what treatment you can get when taking time off from work.

Chapter 13

"The Unexamined Life Is Not Worth Liing"

- Socrates

Philosophy

What is Philosophy:

The study of the basic ideas about knowledge, truth, right and wrong, religion, and the nature and meaning of life.

Merriam-Webster Dictionary

Ancient Greece was considered the home of philosophy. Their quotes and examination of life help us better understand our world.

Socrates:

An Ancient Greek philosopher who lived from 470 to 399 BC for about 71 years.

He is considered the father of Western philosophy and helped develop moral and ethical forms of philosophy. The following quotes are attributed to being recorded by his student, Plato, as

Socrates didn't write anything down.

> *"To know is to know that you know nothing.
> That is the true meaning of knowledge."*
>
> – **Socrates**

When you are young, you think you are on top of the world in developing your career. We think we know everything and are arrogant. You are working hard, and at first, you don't recognize the negative feelings of depression. Before you know it, you are plunged into the darkness where all you can think about is harming yourself or others. You need to realize that you don't know anything about depression or mental illness and need to get help and develop skills to survive.

> *"It is not living that matters, but living rightly."*
>
> – **Socrates**

When dealing with mental health issues, you will want to know how best to treat them with medication, counseling, and developing coping skills. Treating a mental illness can be a long journey, as medication can take months to reach the proper therapeutic level to help reduce your symptoms. Develop healthy coping skills to help reduce the symptoms. I provided chapters on appropriate eating and exercise to help reduce the symptoms. It comes down to what healthy

skills you can develop and find the best combination to help you. Unhealthy developments can range from overeating, causing excessive weight gain, and seeking vices like alcohol and

addictive drugs like heroin or cocaine to help you cope. Always discuss any options with your mental health specialist to help you better develop a plan of action.

> *"Falling down is not a failure. Failure comes when you stay where you have fallen."*
>
> — **Socrates**

Developing mental health issues can quickly feel like you have fallen in life. Luckily, our society has a wealth of medical and counseling resources to help you cope and improve your mental health. Having a family that understands your situation can go a long way to helping you in the long run. Recovering from a mental illness can be a long journey, but knowing that you have a problem is the first step.

Plato

Born around 428 B.C., he lived for about 70 to 80 years and is considered the central figure in Western philosophy. Plato is why we have all the teachings of Socrates and similar philosophers, as he wrote down the teachings so we can study them today. He also founded the Platonic Academy, the first school of philosophy.

> *"There are two things a person should never be angry at: what they can help and cannot."*
>
> — *Plato*

Politics is the best example because I wrote this book in late 2024. The most significant influence we have in politics is when we can vote. Once the candidate is elected, we can try to influence them by calling them or sending letters, but in the end, the politicians can decide. Their bad decisions can affect their re-election, but that doesn't happen for 2 - 6 years, depending on their office.

We can't choose our parents or our genetics in life. It is pointless to express anger if we are upset with how our minds and bodies developed as children. We can work hard to keep our bodies in shape and study hard in school, but ultimately, we all hit a wall regarding what we can achieve.

I would have loved to be an astronaut or something similar to live out my Star Trek fantasy or help with leaving this planet. With the combination of my mental illness and barely being able to pass my advanced math classes, that dream won't be possible.

As children, we are all told that we can be anything we want to be, but if I can't grasp quantum mechanics, I won't be the next Albert Einstein.

Once you can accept the world around you and understand what you can do to improve your circumstances and the world around you, you can plan for your success.

"Nothing beautiful without struggle"

— Plato

Everyone experiences a constant struggle throughout life. You can only control how you deal with and overcome the battle. When dealing with mental illness, the key is to quickly find the best resources, medication, and counselor to help them cope.

"All is flux, nothing stays still."

— Plato

The only constant in life is change, as nothing stays the same. We will all experience hardship and strife, especially when dealing with a mental illness. Finding the correct way to implement that change will always result in a better life and a chance of meeting your goals.

What Does It Mean:

Like exploring philosophy, you will want to explore the causes and solutions of your struggles. Scholars have studied psychology, the mind, and the meaning of happiness throughout the centuries.

Chapter 14

"Thou shouldst eat to live; not live to eat"

— *Socrates / Benjamin Franklin*

Neuro Diet:

Please discuss any significant changes to your diet or supplements with your family doctor before making any significant changes.

Your daily diet goes a long way toward helping you produce the neurotransmitters your mind needs to survive.

A poor diet can prevent the body from getting the resources it needs to maintain a balanced mental state. What diet will hurt your mental state, and what kind will help it? Again, please discuss any supplements or changes in your diet with your family doctor before making any significant changes.

The Negative Mental Health Diet

1. Red Processed Meats
2. Refined Grains Like White Bread
3. Simple Carbs and Sugars
    a. Candy
    b. Junk Food
4. High-Fat Meats

5. Low Intake of Fruits & Vegetables

Eating right may seem common sense, but remember:

Common Sense Is So Rare. It's A God Damn Superpower

— *PZ Meyer*

The Pro-Mental Health Diet:

1. Fruits
2. Vegetables
3. Whole Grain
4. Fish
5. Lean Meats Like Poultry
6. Low-Fat Dairy
7. Olive Oil

We now know what to eat; the question is why.

What kind of food is related to helping your mental health?

Vitamin D:

Low Vitamin D levels may impair cognitive function and reduce Serotonin because there are vitamin D receptors in areas of the brain responsible for mood and behavior, including depression. (7)

Good Sources of Vitamin D

1. Get More Sunlight

2. Fatty Fish & Seafood
3. Mushrooms
4. Egg Yolks
5. Eat fortified foods like Breakfast Cereal
6. UV Lamps
7. Dairy Milk
8. Almond Milk

Sunlight Lamps

Getting outside can be difficult simply because most activities require being inside. When dealing with depression and anxiety, the motivation to even go outside when it is not needed can be complex. I invested in a natural sunlight bulb for my reading lamp.

Speaking from experience, I significantly improved my mood when I started using a sun lamp and kept it on for most of my day.

Carbs And Serotonin:

Carbohydrates are foods consisting of or containing many sugars, starches, cellulose, or similar substances broken down to release energy in the human body. They are one of the leading nutritional food groups.

Carbohydrates give your body the fuel it needs to function; a lot of that energy also goes to Serotonin production and mood stabilization. (8)

Recommended Foods:

1. Whole Grains
2. Complex Carbs
3. Avoid Simple Sugars And Sweets.

Good Source of Whole Grains:

1. Whole Oats
2. Whole Wheat
3. Whole-Grain Rye
4. Buckwheat
5. Brown Rice
6. Corn
7. Popcorn
8. Whole Grain Bread.

Good Sources of Complex Carbs:

1. Apples
2. Oranges
3. Banana
4. Peaches
5. Peas
6. Brown Rice
7. Whole Grain Pasta

8. Corn
9. Peas

Protein's Effects On Serotonin & Dopamine:

Protein

Proteins like meat comprise chemical 'building blocks' called amino acids. Your body uses amino acids to build and repair muscles and bones and to make hormones and enzymes. They can also be utilized as an energy source. (9)

Amino Acids:

Amino acids combine to form proteins. Amino acids and proteins are the building blocks of life.

When proteins are digested or broken down, amino acids are the result. The human body then uses amino acids to make proteins to help the body break down food.

A diet high in protein provides the building blocks of amino acids that help produce the Neurotransmitters Serotonin & Dopamine. (10)

Recommended Foods:

1. Lean Poultry
2. Fish
3. Seeds & Nuts

Tryptophan Essential Amino Acid:

It is an amino acid needed for average growth and the production and maintenance of the body's proteins, muscles, enzymes, and neurotransmitters.

Tryptophan's Essential Amino Acid:

Recommended Sources:

1. Chicken
2. Eggs
3. Fish
4. Cheese
5. Peanuts
6. Pumpkin & Sesame Seeds
7. Turkey
8. Milk
9. Tofu & Soy

Chapter 15

"Happiness consists of getting enough sleep."

- ***Irish Proverb***

Sleep & Mental Health

Getting enough sleep has a significant effect on your mental health, regardless of whether you have a diagnosed mental illness. (21)

It may seem like common sense, but please see the quote in the diet section regarding common sense. The consensus is getting around 6 - 8 hours of uninterrupted sleep.

One thing that mental illness and depression can cause is that you sleep too much or too little, and making sure you get a maximum of 6 - 8 hours of sleep is essential.

You can use alarms and tell your parents or roommates to get up after a specific time each day. Considering that we are a nation of screen time, the idea is to stop watching TV and put away your smartphone at least one hour before bed. The easiest thing to do then is to read a physical book.

A healthy snack before bed, such as a piece of fruit, seeds, or nuts, can also help. My favorite is listening to my favorite podcast about movie reviews as I lie down, which gets me asleep quickly.

Showering or bathing before bed can also help; the hot water can relax and help you sleep. There are a lot of over-the-counter and prescription sleep options.

Sleep medicine is another area where I would recommend talking to your family doctor first, as they can harm you if you take too much. Considering any suicidal tendencies, you should avoid them.

Chapter 16

"Running allows you to see how wonderful your life is."

- Kara Goucher

Chasing the Runners' High

Do you ever notice that after a long walk, a bike ride, or similar exercise, you may experience a sensation of happiness, calmness, and reduced pain levels?

Do you ever wonder what causes all these sensations in the body?

Just 20 - 60 minutes of cardio exercise 3 - 5 days a week can positively affect your mood.

While exercising, your brain releases the Endocannabinoid neurotransmitter, which produces the sensation of happiness, calmness, and reduced pain levels. (5)

The Endocannabinoid neurotransmitter is related to THC and marijuana.

Chapter 17

"Rule your mind or it will rule you"

- *Buddha*

Meditation & Mindfulness:

"A growing body of research shows that mindfulness can decrease stress, increase mental and physical health and cognitive functioning, and improve performance and well-being. As a result, several organizations have started implementing mindfulness programs for their employees."

- *Hyland et al., 2015, p. 595 (20)*

Considering that I grew up in a culture of action and martial arts movies, I would typically see my favorite hero going through a training montage. It would very often show them meditating before a fight. This meditation got me wondering how something so simple as sitting still for a short time can make a difference in your life.

My meditation experience started when I joined a local Buddhist Meditation group in my town. I found meditation took the edge off my mental health issues.

The scientific community has extensively studied meditation, showing it is not just a new-age fad. The question is not whether you should meditate, but what benefits you will gain from taking 10 minutes to undergo a guided meditation.

Meditation:

A mental exercise that scientifically helps your brain.

Meditation is a practice that involves focusing or clearing one's mind using a combination of psychological and physical techniques. Depending on the type of meditation, one can relax and reduce anxiety and stress.

The average meditation only takes 10 minutes in a quiet location. We all have 10 minutes of free time in our busy day.

Let's Jump In:

Search YouTube.com for

Mindfulness Bell - A 5-Minute Mindfulness Meditation:

By The Guided Meditation Site Channel.

You will want to sit in a quiet place and play the video. You should concentrate on your breathing during the meditation. Come back once you have watched the video:

That sensation you are now experiencing is a quieting of the mind and a better sense of centering yourself. This simple exercise has been extensively researched and positively correlates with your mind.

Meditation Research:

They have found unexpected improvements in the brain from just eight weeks of regular meditation. (14)

They have seen significant changes in the

1. Amygdala
2. Hippocampus

The Science After 8 Weeks Of Meditation Amygdala:

The gray matter related to the Amygdala decreases. Reducing the gray matter can significantly improve your anxiety and help you build confidence over time.

Hippocampus

The gray matter associated with the Hippocampus has increased, which can improve your memory and learning skills.

Moments of Unexplained Happiness:

They also found that the participants described more random moments when they felt happier overall. (15)

Slow Your Roll:

Meditation helps slow down the neural network of wandering thoughts. It helps slow down your mind's wandering to help you stay focused during your daily life. (18)

Pain Don't Hurt:

Chronic pain doctors have used meditation as a method to increase the pain threshold. (17)

Focus:

Meditation is known for helping you reduce the ability to get distracted and get back on task when distracted. (18)

Improve Serotonin Levels:

Meditation has a positive correlation with reducing cortisol neurotransmitters and improving your levels of Serotonin. (16)

Music and Dopamine: I Want To Rock!

Do you ever wonder why you enjoy your favorite rock band or country music? We all have our favorite musical style to enjoy alone or with others.

Studies show that music, along with medication, lifestyle changes, and nutrition, has a positive correlation with improving dopamine levels. (19)

Chapter 18

"Let endings be the stepping stones to your adventure's dawn"

- *Unknown*

Your Personal 12 Trials To Recovery

Being someone who has suffered from depression for all my adult life, I can say that it has harmed my life. Thankfully, I was living in a time when depression and bipolar disorders were treatable, and some services helped me recover. Can I say that I wish I had never developed this disorder and would prefer the everyday life my brother and sister enjoy? Unfortunately, I have been dealt these cards and need to play them to the best of my ability.

Whenever we experience a hardship in our lives, we all have 12 trials to overcome that hardship. When it comes to mental illness, we should all have the essential three trials to start with.

1. Talk to a mental health professional.
2. Start with mental health talk therapy.
3. Seek mental health medical intervention.

You will need to find out what the subsequent nine trials are for your journey to recovery. The fact that you are reading this book means you have questions or concerns regarding depression and your mental health issues. With some luck, you have gotten a better handle on how mental health affects your body, and being able to cope with it on top of medical interventions will help you thrive in your life.

Ultimately, we are all heroes of our own story, and it is just a matter of finding our path to glory and immortality. Like every hero's journey, you must overcome hardships and tragedies and manage your path to victory. In the end, you only fail if you give up on yourself.

Chapter 19

"Ignorance makes it too easy to jump to conclusions."

- Robin Wall Kimmerer

In Conclusion,

Knowledge is power, and knowing how to improve your mind has no limits to what you can do. This information is designed to work with medical interventions such as medication and counseling.

We all suffer, and what we do about that ultimately matters. In the end, remember this little wisdom:

Dying Is Easy, Living Is Hard.

So start living and prove to yourself and the world that you are not your diagnosis, and you will not allow your mental illness to be the end of you.

Chapter 20

"You can't understand a person until you've walked a mile in their shoes."

- Mary T. Lathrap

About The Author

Chris Strauss suffers from bipolar I, has experienced multiple depressive and manic states, and is a suicide survivor. He has his share of good and bad days dealing with his mental illness. His worst suicide attempt involved driving his car into a maple tree. He has a bachelor's degree in social work and a minor in psychology. Being a geek would be the best way to describe him, as he always wants to talk about the latest Marvel or Star Wars movies to no end. He currently lives in Wisconsin near friends and family.

References

Hamilton JP, Siemer M, Gotlib IH. Amygdala volume in major depressive disorder: a meta-analysis of magnetic resonance imaging studies. Mol Psychiatry. 2008 Nov;13(11):993-1000. Doi: 10.1038/mp 2008.57. Epub 2008 May 27. PMID: 18504424; PMCID: PMC2739676.

Darren W. Roddy, Chloe Farrell, Kelly Doolin, Elena Roman, Leonardo Tozzi, Thomas Frodl, Veronica O'Keane, Erik O'Hanlon, The Hippocampus in Depression: More Than the Sum of Its Parts? Advanced Hippocampal Substructure Segmentation in Depression, Biological Psychiatry, Volume 85, Issue 6, 2019, Pages 487-497, ISSN 0006-3223

Kaczkurkin AN, Foa EB. Cognitive-behavioral therapy for anxiety disorders: an update on the empirical evidence. Dialogues Clin Neurosci. 2015 Sep;17(3):337- 46. doi: 10.31887/DCNS.2015.17.3/akaczkurkin. PMID: 26487814; PMCID: PMC4610618.

Fenger-Grøn M, Kjaersgaard MIS, Parner ET, Guldin MB, Vedsted P, Vestergaard M. Early treatment with talk therapy or antidepressants in severely bereaved people and risk of suicidal behavior and psychiatric illness: an instrumental variable analysis. Clin Epidemiol. 2018 Aug 24;10:1013-1026. Doi: 10.2147/CLEP.S157996. PMID: 30197539; PMCID: PMC6112782.

David A. Raichlen, Adam D. Foster, Gregory L. Gerdeman, Alexandre Seillier, Andrea Giuffrida; Wired to run: exercise-induced endocannabinoid signaling in humans and cursorial mammals with implications for the 'runner's high.' J Exp Biol 15 April 2012; 215 (8): 1331–1336. doi: https://doi.org/10.1242/jeb.063677

Selvaraj R, Selvamani TY, Zahra A, Malla J, Dhanoa RK, Venugopal S, Shoukrie SI, Hamouda RK, Hamid P. Association Between Dietary Habits and Depression: A Systematic Review. Cureus. 2022 Dec 9;14(12):e32359. doi: 10.7759/cureus 32359. PMID: 36632273; PMCID: PMC9828042.

Akpınar Ş, Karadağ MG. Is Vitamin D Important in Anxiety or Depression? What Is the Truth? Curr Nutr Rep. 2022 Dec;11(4):675-681. doi: 10.1007/s13668-022-00441-0. Epub 2022 Sep 13. PMID: 36097104; PMCID: PMC9468237.

Wurtman RJ, Wurtman JJ. Brain serotonin, carbohydrate-craving, obesity, and depression. Obes Res. 1995 Nov;3 Suppl 4:477S-480S. Doi: 10.1002/j.1550-8528.1995.tb00215.x. PMID: 8697046.

Microbes Yunting Xie, Chong Wang, Di Zhao, Chao Wang, and Chunbao Li. Dietary Proteins Regulate Serotonin Biosynthesis and Catabolism by the Specific Gut. Journal of Agricultural and Food Chemistry 2020 68 (21), 5880-5890 DOI: 10.1021/acs.jafc.0c00832

Umeda K, Shindo D, Somekawa S, Nishitani S, Sato W, Toyoda S, Karakawa S, Kawasaki M, Mine T, Suzuki K. Effects of Five Amino Acids (Serine, Alanine, Glutamate, Aspartate, and Tyrosine) on Mental

Health in Healthy Office Workers: A Randomized, Double-Blind, Placebo-Controlled Exploratory Trial. Nutrients. 2022 Jun 6;14(11):2357. doi: 10.3390/nu14112357. PMID: 35684157; PMCID: PMC9183184.

(1) Sangle P, Sandhu O, Aftab Z, Anthony AT, Khan S. Vitamin B12 Supplementation: Preventing Onset and Improving Prognosis of Depression. Cureus. 2020 Oct 26;12(10):e11169. doi: 10.7759/cureus.11169. PMID: 33251075; PMCID: PMC7688056.

(2) Wang J, Um P, Dickerman BA, Liu J. Zinc, Magnesium, Selenium, and Depression: A Review of the Evidence, Potential Mechanisms, and Implications. Nutrients. 2018 May 9;10(5):584. doi: 10.3390/nu10050584. PMID: 29747386; PMCID: PMC5986464.

(3) Schachter HM, Kourad K, Merali Z, et al. Effects of Omega-3 Fatty Acids on Mental Health: Summary. 2005 Jul. In: AHRQ Evidence Report Summaries. Rockville (MD): Agency for Healthcare Research and Quality (US); 1998-2005. 116. Available from:

https://www.ncbi.nlm.nih.gov/books/NBK11853/

(4) McGee, M. Meditation and Psychiatry. Psychiatry (Edgmont). 2008 Jan;5(1):28-41. PMID: 19727302; PMCID: PMC2719544.

(5) Matthew A. Killingsworth, Daniel T. Gilbert, A Wandering Mind Is an Unhappy Mind.Science330,932- 932(2010).DOI:10.1126/science.1192439

(6) John J. Miller, Ken Fletcher, Jon Kabat-Zinn, Three-year follow-up and clinical implications of a mindfulness meditation-based stress reduction intervention in the treatment of anxiety disorders, General Hospital Psychiatry, Volume 17, Issue 3,1995, Pages 192-200, ISSN 0163-8343,

(7) Zeidan F, Martucci KT, Kraft RA, Gordon NS, McHaffie JG, Coghill RC. Brain mechanisms supporting the modulation of pain by mindfulness meditation. J Neurosci. 2011 Apr 6;31(14):5540- 8. doi: 10.1523/JNEUROSCI.5791-10.2011. PMID: 21471390; PMCID: PMC3090218.

(8) Jamil A, Gutlapalli SD, Ali M, Oble MJP, Sonia SN, George S, Shahi SR, Ali Z, Abaza A, Mohammed L. Meditation and Its Mental and Physical Health Benefits in 2023. Cureus. 2023 Jun 19;15(6):e40650. doi: 10.7759/cureus 40650. PMID: 37476142; PMCID: PMC10355843.

(9) Gebauer, L., Kringelbach, M. L., & Vuust, P. (2012). Ever-changing cycles of musical pleasure: The role of dopamine and anticipation. Psychomusicology: Music, Mind, and Brain, 22(2), 152–167. https://doi.org/10.1037/a0031126

(10) Hyland PK, Lee RA, Mills MJ. Mindfulness at Work: A New Approach to Improving Individual and Organizational Performance. Industrial and Organizational Psychology. 2015;8(4):576-602. doi:10.1017/iop.2015.41

(11) Blackwelder A, Hoskins M, Huber L. Effect of Inadequate Sleep on Frequent Mental Distress. Prev Chronic Dis

2021;18:200573. DOI: https://doi.org/10.5888/ pcd18.200573.

www.ingramcontent.com/pod-product-compliance
Lightning Source LLC
Chambersburg PA
CBHW050249010526
44107CB00003B/249